THROUGH
DISASSEMBLED
HOUSES
OF
PERFECT
STONES

WINNIPEG

DAVID YEREX WILLIAMSON

THROUGH
DISASSEMBLED
HOUSES
OF
PERFECT
STONES

Through Disassembled Houses of Perfect Stones

Copyright © 2022 David Yerex Williamson

Published by At Bay Press March 2022.

ISBN 978-1-988168-60-9

Library and Archives Canada cataloguing in publication is available
upon request.

Printed and bound in Canada.

This book is printed on acid free paper that is 100% recycled ancient
forest friendly (100% post-consumer recycled).

First Edition

10 9 8 7 6 5 4 3 2 1

atbaypress.com

ACKNOWLEDGEMENTS

My sincere thanks to Jonathon Ball, Lauren Carter, and Ariel Gordon, The League of Canadian Poets, and the Manitoba Writers Guild. I want to acknowledge the support and encouragement of editors Oz Hardwick, Lesley Strutt, Lori Cayer, Anne Burke, Barbara Carter, Madison Stoner, Barbara Schott, Yvonne Blomer, Joan Conway, Blaine Marchad, Jennifer Still, and Chelene Knight. Thanks also to Lorri Nielsen Glenn for her kindness and insights, and to Duncan Mercredi for his words and his spirit.

I want to thank Matt Joudrey for his support and to Karen Clavelle for her keen eye and for keeping my voice intact.

I extend my appreciation to Dr. Dan Smith of University College of the North for his support.

Poet's photo credit, Bruce Folster © 2020.

…

Poems in this collection have appeared in the publications Aesthetica Magazine's *International Creative Writing Annual, The Antigonish Review, The Broken Spine* (UK), *Contemporary Verse 2, Heartwood: Poems for the Love of Trees, The Dalhousie Review, Mojave He(Art) Review, The New Quarterly, Prairie Fire, Overture: A Canadian Anthology of New Poetry, Prairie Journal of Canadian Literature, Sweet Water: Poems for the Watersheds, Tower Poetry, Winnipeg Free Press National Poetry Month feature,* 49.8.

In memory of
Mavis Margaret (Yerex) Williamson
(1936 – 2006)

and
Stanley George (Pee Wee) Sinclair
(1929 – 2015)

and
for their descendants

Layer after layer of autumn leaves
are swept away
Something forgets us perfectly

– Leonard Cohen

CONTENTS

FROST CRUSTED POPLAR

Following the erosion
cracked imagery on crooked page
I snowshoe to the mouth
of the river past
the crisp site the fox patrols
past the comfort of language past
the abandoned trading post
graveyard of starved Cree past
no words
sounds
through sites of empty names
still air through tamarack-blank
drifts between jack pine
my tongue a rock
starving my own mouth
worn
I pause against a frost-crusted poplar
shifting weight
tighten my stance
my ungloved fingers thaw
thin smooth grooves in her old skin
what memory communes in her pulp
when she last felt lonely human
hands
pressing flesh
young snows reclaim
the lines left which lead
me here

figures grafting meaning to silence
a breeze startled snow off one branch
her roots nudging me
home old tracks towards a new page –
the wind whistles through the gaps in me
her own crumpled poem

53° 59' 37" N 97° 48' 41" W

Our airport is small, smells
slightly of burnt fabric insulation.
Sometimes planes don't land.
Doctors stay another night
far from Thai restaurants, their children, jazz.
Here, it snows in April
and May. Sometimes June. Usually September.
We have no insurance agent.
Truck registration renewals go out by plane,
sometimes, return in a box to be retrieved
or left. Dozens of envelopes waiting over nights.
I note the names of people
with whom to avoid collisions.

The old HBC fort a national historic site now
we have to send our future out to be born,
our elderly to die. Between,
sometimes we garden, dust off the tools,
retrieve from the soil, snare or angle our meat
when the river strands us as well.
We hope for specific change,
seasons clinging to a coming today.

Once the ferry re-opens, we have the usual dreams:
well-attended funerals, a new rumour
maybe a Thai place dimly lit
a dark-eyed waiter who doesn't yet know your name.
I could mail myself Air

but here, if the ferry runs,
I would leave by truck
spend the day grounded, Tom T. Hall on the radio,
arrive dusty, late, out of sorts –
much like I departed.

Sometimes our planes don't land.
Most days we have running water.
We have no train station. No theatre.

Above us, ravens pause in the wind,
shadow the snow.

WINTER ROAD

April reminds us
        the river is not made of stone
She is more than winter roads   to bring the outside in
February yawns
       through
                March-shudders
       tomorrows melt-sink
  the high way
dissolves the inside left
out

Old ice-drifts
freed   into another season
young water coaxing us
      to roam
longing unmapped journeys to   stretch
  through boreal branches
        ancestor breezes
        sing
stories the land collected
before others called them
       history

Under dancing green shimmers
glistened ripples
       tap the old skin   of night
       on shores

          lakes with empty names
spring
in shallow breathes
a season of change
a season of   same

the inside
               out
the river   free

April reminds us

LIGHTS HOME FOR DAUGHTER

11:05 pm: escape is more than crossing rivers
septembering nowhere towns
more than unknotting cutter scars under lace gloves
more than Jerome's hash pipe
in your knapsack
less than his guitar silent in your closet

2:09 am: back home buzzing stars blind
to a crescent moon by taking root
in dirt black sky
golden green night whispers dance
before tamarack orange autumn truth
the fall like childhood
change spent south

3:51 am: Kookum's paper Jesus bookmark
a fifty-dollar bill, dried tiger lilies
pressed into Cohen
Highway 6 south of 53°
half-white grey gosling
spinning your hours away
in a travelling neighbourhood
everyone is homeless
hoping perhaps the next stop
may claim you

5:55 am: begging others your quiet
these southern trees wear different costumes
hide in unfinished
summer's dance
sleepy sunrises
this road a life prayer
you – blood river collected
in bone-bowl memory
more than a rope loophole
for a guitar-playing boy named Jerome
his breath whispers
clinging to your coat tails still

8:25 am: *I need to know home, you text me*

LEARNING MY OWN BODY

Somewhere between these words
lies my mother's faith
a benign lump
nestled in an obscure fold of flesh
       undetonated

She wouldn't have liked that
air of the sinister
that can never work its way out
of this version of this poem
       yet

I am an anatomy of others
inhabited, in some parts
by my mother's rustic order
her particular way
Nothing held a specific place
       even in verse

Leaves unraked, another duty missed
abandoned to November's meagre snow
on my mother's last morning
I drive too late by her childhood church
       her moment passed

My mother refused to be an actor
in her own death but I
this smoothing rough edges
        a kind of devotion:
I record as it resides in me

A spectre lingering in the vacated cavity
heart's empty chambers
carelessly fingers line in the dust
reminding me of the slow neglect of faith, of flesh
        of memory I am slowly learning to pearl
my mother's marrow mapped beneath my bones

AT THE PIANO IN GRANDMOTHER'S FRONT ROOM

Small hands accompany mine
gracing knuckles shadow keys
One verse summons
the origins of the next like the song
in an ancestral letter
            passed lips to lips to lips
grandmother to father to daughter
as the day ushers night
no note holding the exact memory

Unlocked music knows no age

Crafting this act of passing
descendant seeds press the shell
shadows of skin
            shedding   shorn
This town our name returns
births new stories
buried bones
born of the land

Today no earth remembers
maps cling to shifting walls,
threads, sewing lines further west
    settled, homesteaded, titled, vacated,
traded   old land
for newer old land

Till your grandfather's story
remains
ground broken, greying stones
collected in corner fields
      of blood dealt
        no history lives in just one story

You remain one place long enough
your past may leave you for another
more suited to memoir –
a song to follow

Hours later in my childhood bedroom
under great-grandmother's crocheted afghan
your fingers sleeping in my beard
    I hear you hum
my fingers trace dead names I smell
in a bible we learned to keep
through disassembled houses
of perfect stones

TAX SALE

In a silent still
among moved pictures
three wrinkled bent
cigarette butts crushed
smoked words yellowed, unfiltered
in a cream-coloured saucer
chipped edges
in *Silver Birch*

Old years steal voice
thick with brandied tea
grandfather sang to his
accordion
on tended land, fading
plank floors, peeling wallpaper
sang through old spice and boiled cabbage
something other than speaking
to shake off the dirt

TOUCH /
STONE

On the 52nd anniversary of my birth
wetting my boots
I picked a small yellow stone
from the Dargle waters
   of Wicklow County

Its absence there fills
an empty pocket here
straddling the boreal forest
wearing my skin as
I tramp   twists in travel

My father's father's father's
family came from Wicklow
I'm not sure what that means

Some days my presence
comes from
                        atoms of the thinnest memory
dwell
in the fissures
        of the earth we mark

On the 53rd anniversary of my birth
these same boots kicked dry
restless leaf-murmur along a ravine
        settle precarious among fragments
of Precambrian shield
I'm uncertain where I came from
or to what stones
I may belong

CARRYING HER SECRET

I touch the pine board
your head leaned
against in 1954
where whispers
you could not terminate
would not take names so
you bore flesh
carried time
obedience beyond belief
and then
you were sent to normal
school alone
in 1954   this
was how it was done

Trailing families
after you passed
we are knotted wood
kin beyond blood
I put away
the shards of grief
meet this half-brother
under his sister's song
sharing our grandfather's eyes
clearer gentler
knowing how it was done
we grasped hands
held in our veins
secrets kept of our mother
how it was
how it is

FALLOW SEASONS

Weeds pulled from inside you
betray soil
tended more carefully than offspring.
Every season grew
larger through
bank letters, quota tickets
piercing hails, no medical insurance
costs of fuel, the price of wheat
autumn thieves.

Each bedroom diminished
smaller by love passed:
dusty words, missed birthdays
spring pageants, daily
breads, rhyming songs
ceremonies of rust, acres of slippage
silos of loss.

Your father hid in bottles
Saturday night hockey
every cleaned ring and carburetor port
a minor god
of small blunt angers
shadowed the wintered night.

Brothers fallowed, leaving
cycles of harrowing undone
acres of broken duties done
distant gestures
remembered after slender rains.

What becomes of me in you
kicking stones you carried
clearing fields.
Will I hold grief worthy
a prayer after leaving, losing
land you tended

ASSEMBLED STONES

Stones do not feel
the long decay of death
loneliness abandoned

stones remain

like the dead
collect small fissures fading grey
buzz of dream husks
littering gravel roads
comforted-remaining
still

NORMALCY

The morning of my father's heart attack
my brother jangled me into another
sleepless Sunday morning
without worship or ritual

The phone connected
that fear of orphaning
planets slowing
paths over growing

He'll be fine in time
in time with changes
that old dog
he'll be back to normal soon

Setting the course for normal
next week, forest fires
chasing us from home

Salvaged memories boxed in a truck
remote calls sorted healing
light touches of voice through ash
squeezing us into scattered normals

SIDING 22

Rooted
by rail line
the wooden barley king
shimmers in August sun straight
and narrow all my
summers
small

If I walk those ties
(or jump a steel hopper)
there is a library in the next town
a cinema, a French girl
and from there . . .

Today
subdivision abandoned,
crows, rusting wheel barrows, lilacs,
torn hinges,
mother's voice calling
empty classrooms, empty buildings

Grandfather
believed you can
only dwell in one house,
walk in one world,
a single language
talks not to the
homeless

 I drew holes
paged my great escape
where every horizon grows local
sky is sky   home was
is   shall be
against the grain

FOUR MILES OUTSIDE THE TOWN LIMITS

She's flooded.

My uncle's '67 Plymouth Fury
318 three-in-the-tree,
charcoal grey, smells of *Old
Sail, 10w30, English Leather*
time spent   smoked dust,
a Stan Rogers' phrase
rusting in the glove box

We'll get her going in jiff.

Neighbours in the fall,
he knew the uncle my dad
their dad and the dad before
drives blue *Chev* truck after blue *Chev* truck
chocolate-covered *Revels*
at fairground ball games
stands stone silent back in the United Church

*318's a good engine. 340, 360,
383, 400, 440 Dodge made a bunch
they'll all get you there
fast enough. 318's lasted.*

I hold the air breather cover,
grey brown fingers spun,
hands me the wing nut,
places the cover on the bent shoulder
by the ditch where his grandson
rolled that *Buick Skyhawk*
graduation night

Gonna stick my finger down her throat
open her up a bit.
Hold down the clutch and turn her over.
Don't give her no gas though.

Giving her no gas I feel
the rise and rumble
she starts

Clutch released
he screwed on the air breather
cover grins, shakes my hand
calls me my uncle's name
the same name
as his grandson

I'll follow you back to town
just to be sure

COOPERING

Coopering CPR boxcars
in August afternoon
outside was 36° C (97 by the old way)
inside the metal container
frames of 1 x 4 discards
hammered scraps from *Beaver Lumber*
stapled corrugated wax-sided cardboard
seal in barley dust
residue of rented land
a lost uncle
his daughter's tuition
collecting in the coopered seams

I climb the frame
across the sliding door
stripped off a drenched t-shirt
stretched the heat out of my shoulders
kneeled on the gangplank
The Sun Also Rises folded in my back pocket
guzzled warm lemonade from a quart sealer
my mother made the night before
stare down the rail line
to nowhere I'd ever been
another presence
in the seams

PAUSE

Others travel
slip through me
mending memory

Old lives attach
to older stones turned,
thrown, dropped
water   uprooted levee
makes home
between the turns
in ground
a river pauses
against
its will

THIS SEASON

Live through each death
getting it wrong
until it becomes our own

Death teaches
very little
how to cup a shattered soul
against our breast
then let it fly
or fall

The old years seep
into an arrangement
like flowers
or breaths
of first kisses

Visit the ruins
of youth
with other promises
than death
such love is not an artifact

Live through each death
getting it wrong
becoming
moving lips
to the end
of a sigh

PALLIATIVE CARE

Peg, dear, you have another card drawn by that granddaughter
of yours. She's a little squish, that one. Let me set it up
on the sill here for you.

In grey October fog
through narrow arms of window
solitary birch
leaves whispered notes
crumbling,
a season losing song

Behind misted pane
windless autumn litter
decays
into silence

Did you want me to close those curtains for you, Peg?
No, no, that's fine, dear. You just relax. I'll leave
them as they are for you.

Wearing thick wet air
birch cries, suffers
winter's ghosts
growing from her open bones
dropping
greying greens, huddle.

Among her gnarled roots,
drops of fallen past
nourishing
shadows in her sleep.

You rest now, Peg. Let me set the shade.

CAPTIVE

Thursday's trap door below her
memory swings and up
climbs the same captor
always that man, grey wool suit,
            red carnation
taking her furniture, pictures,
Saturdays' hostage
again she bumps into
spaces between bare walls
of personal care

Tuesday teaspoons clatter around
pronouns and prepositions,
turn against her
it's all for and him
            from, and, to, and she
under
always them
Sundays standing in shaky dark,
her shadow pulled from within
by that child, Is that green corduroy?
she can't place
strangers in framed thens

Wednesday's worn thin metal circles
round her bent finger
she turns and strokes warm
            its edges

                        remembers
little from where it came
only that touching it
keeps Monday quiet
and the smile less
foreign, younger
almost
Friday
grey and red
            and

WEARING YOUR PAST

Morning stretches, rubs her sleepy eyes.
I release words like smoke or tears
to mark the days.
It is quiet in the house
the radio's light hum of old roots
nudges the hours through flickering leaves
a same-lazy breeze.

Morning stretches, arcs her tired back.
Flies buzz small collisions
with the screen door
a cold tea cup on the bench
three sea shells on a prairie sill.
The photo tells me your eyes
were the red brown of burnt cinnamon.

Morning stretches, her small hands open.
I cannot remember things I read
last month, two, three times.
I know there is another world
a second life, somewhere we are,
I believe this is not, I know, forever.
Cold tea in cup on the bench.

Morning stretches, her face to the sun.
I think I smell the shade of your hair
in the cracks of the room
bits of more words scatter
along the hardwood into corners
some of the syllables I hear
like the last line of a novel
I know but don't

SUNDANCE

Fifteen-two fifteen-four fifteen-six
and a pair's eight
right Jack makes nine
drops your hand

We play next to a garden
of bones, copper plates, stone heads
the empty theatre languishing
strand across the alley
your grandfather's bakery
sold, boarded up

It wasn't a great run but
still
you smile
if you write about this
let me be Sundance
he got the girl

In this journey
cells dissolve, move pictures
        voices in the trees
say they know you
    yes, I nod
They aren't lying but
it's only half the tale

You peel the thick rind
of orange for tea
wink, as I collect my hand
nineteen points I nod
you smile

Always
in this verse
you get the girl

I throw my hand

#11

After midnight weeds glisten
but their language is different
from the stars
the red metal bridge
to the rest of me
hangs to-night by
a river
your eulogy

You, falling sound
spirit dark
mumbling child games
distance
pains
the cellars of boyhood
in our brothers' clothes
hockey father's different labours
baker's boy, grain buyer's son,
we stole
Crown Royal and *Export A*
for the goal line
after practice

Between stones
I drive
five hundred miles
through dark tree silence
I speak
after the service
your mother cradled
my nerve endings slipped
me back into my body
her sad smile
soft purple weight
on my cheek

I flew back
off shore, dozed
to old sounds of cold
blades carving ice
wood-slap, sharp-metal clink
arms raised, fading
in a grey frozen sky

FIVE SUMMER DAYS IN THE CITY
(for Audie)

My father sold the house
he lived in with our mother
after 12 years alone
At 87, found space
he could be like he was
in the silver frame that keeps them still

Audie is grey, 83 pounds
dying of cancer for the third time
a tired joke settled in her deep eyes
she touches the sill her laugh
a chorus of green leaves,
the window lets in July air, heavy
thick with smoke from a northern fire

Ping interrupts – another text
as I wheel my niece through the park –
Denny on the streets again
Kamloops last week, Calgary before
his disability ran out, at 56
he will not retire, promises
he will stay moving another summer

After 34 years of teaching my wife
retired, our house needs painting
she tries her best to love an aging husband
our daughter wrestles with shadows

but she finished the term
and the grass was cut

Before these five days are forgotten
I place an old watch in a drawer
beside the stones I collect
for weight to give me ground
grass cut, term complete
I try my best
to be loved

* Audie passed away three days after this poem was completed.

FIT

I slide my hands into
brown suede gloves
from the pockets of that old
green windbreaker
hanging under the stairs
by your golf clubs
tight, but they will fit
adjust in time
warm to changes
in touch

REMISS

You break,
enter with intent,
sink gnarled claws into pure flesh
between the ribs
below the cover of skin,
embers moving under ground –
smoldering along roots
to flare up elsewhere,
startling another sleeping instrument.
You invade and we identify the masses –
real life distinct and separate.
It makes little difference.
It makes all the difference.

Therapy, a scorched-earth policy –
body playing alchemy against itself,
hoping you may take bait.
You suffer such gambles gladly –
bear a scornful grin.
We practice: block, feint, parry,
midnight shadow boxing
just a murmur through the body,
melting snow barely freezing deep pains.
A sponge bath becomes an act of love –
one of few – real life draws beauty in war
much closer than romance in peace.

School bake sales missed, art shows, a concert –
real life slips between fingers – sometimes.
Mornings filled with old songs pass, then
You exit without ceremony, maybe,
leave your bill, your scent, your prints
deep in the debris of structure.
Faint smoke smell hangs –
your corrupt genesis interrupted,
stalled, complete   over.

We pause – unlock doors, windows –
scrub the memory clean,
lie awake
and wonder.

WHERE THE RADIO FADES

Passing Devil's Lake
the machinery of voice
slips below song's architecture
leaving a scratching river
torn golden fields
fallen raspberries dried
lessons of paper
trees kneeling
over dots of ink

I guide my truck past
songs
only the dead
can hear
smoke trails behind
a flat prairie horizon
that left me
before I left it

LOST MEMORY

You are away from home
your childhood edges
buttered in dust and sun

So you clean – routine,
rite, ritual, relief
another Saturday morning
fear, more than dysfunction
toils the laundry
today collides
with yesterday – shadows
spill through
fingers longing for
one last touch
something   forgets
you clean, you clean you
clean you cry

UNDATED

I lied when we met
said it wouldn't be a date
you could remain
you – as if that bird were up to us,
the smooth curve
of occupying each other's language
a breathless
new thing

You grew up without running
water by water carried by hand
words invisible seasons
needed no signs
for change

I kept water in a metal bottle
believed stories
begin outside
ourselves telling
in black scratchings only

So we
navigated boundaries
until one territory
loosened into each other
inhabited
remains' ache

Old we grow
together

DROPPED THREADS

November wind rattles
nights swelling   you occupied
by two souls
flutter pulses   becoming
bed ridden things
to heal   you needed to heal, rest
sipped red rose tea
smoothing the wrinkles
around your belly like we knew what
                          we were doing

To do something,
I started the shopping –
          planning menus, making lists –
have never stopped   for decades   now,
the *Northwest Company Store, IGA*

The darkness
                          scraps in the woods
changed things

February – no midwife:
you were sent south.
We were sent south
    separately
    to smooth the wrinkles

A day breaks open,
new spirit revealed
old words make new space

There was no way to ask
to save the placenta,
to plant what we were –
residues of her,
      remains of us

March, sewn
in cradled fingers,
passengers within histories
to follow   hymns for her

Rain makes her own story
drops weighted to clear away
the old stains
I utter her name
finger the tangled moonlight

Morning
dissolves
            into
            new rituals
      of
us

FROM THE WOMB

Your mother's tongue caresses the woods
shades of moss, pine, tamarack winds
weaving blended light into song.

I kick my words around vacant lots
roll them in clustered dirt and broken sticks
bounce them off cracked shadows.

Your mother's language nourishes
ballads, old men, children,
carries metaphors through
histories like a red willow branch.

My English wars with itself,
paper screams dragged kicking,
between bruised words,
leaving frantic claw marks
on a page.

Your mother's voice may pass
in the arms of her own grandchild.
Mine seeps, at first a dot of blood,
stains natal soil, marks time,
waits to settle, to spread.

TAX CREDIT

December dog piled on the bed
winter-rescued strays all of us
spreads into a glazed sky early
air press against glass
in the woodstove an ember
breaks open its thaw

Terms on the back step incomplete,
tonight is about warming cold hands
home, cracked but safe
other darknesses not spoken
not vanished

Scraped knees, elbows –
among us you fold
your paper wings I draw
mom reading eloquent quiet
truths, wishes
whispered healings

The littlest wolf buries
a nose in my side
I smell cinnamon
glance at the bed stand
opened pastries
French coffee

Mom and I got our bonus from the band
a hundred each
    – Dad tax… I reach
Hey, this is our Indian money
    – I know and as a white man
    it's my job to try to –
Awas, you can't colonize me
in my own home

Impish head rests
littlest wolf paws stretch
both against me, warm gentle
pushing back
slightly

TELLING STONES

You bear the heavy hole
of unlearned language
that acquired barrier
of transient words

Your travelled soul
tripped over legends
tried   told
syllables blunt, inanimate
vowels shrink
dissolve into airless cold
nameless days sobbed out

Staring into the fire
auntie brushed your hair
strum singing
small pebbles
click into story
between the littlest sounds
your heart learns
to hear

BLUE

Gentle folds
in fading grass begin to golden
sky forgets yesterday's prairie blue
lent, still
remains within

The old house is tired
the mice and moths are not

Your skinny fair-haired boy
with suitcase carries loss
in an old beard
extra weight, scant lines
a bootprint in dirt
the leaning house
no longer
recognizes

SUBMISSION

In northern lumber towns
poets do not suffer
crippling self-doubt,
fear of rejection,
long silences between
appearances in journals:
no one we know reads.

We burn our days –
weigh the ashes,
but with wood to cut,
navigate self-publishing services
layers of narratives'
long hours between libraries.

The call of the wild offers
no small romances.
Write or don't write. That is all.
Muses shiver,
complain the wool itches.
The light slants,
it just takes too long to be rejected.

The north calls for our words:
battered we give them all
and wait
for small change

LUPINE SPRING

Three dry weeks in elemental May
single wolf wanders this side of the island
sleighting between rising birch
reclining rock revealing wonder
she slips through low brush
through the dark
into the yard
curious of our dogs
they yip and kneel
dodge and dart low moans
revive some ancient canine ritual

she rolls through the grass
her teats engorged
cubs perhaps hidden nearby
or maybe dead
leaves secrets for
the cool rising moon mist
holding her breaths

POETRY READING
R.D. Parker Collegiate

This is today's line
tethered by words
dropped out of yesterday's mouth.

This is today's line.
Polished, it will glow,
make me hundreds,
change the world.

This is today's line.
Please remain behind the velvet rope.
Hold your applause until the end.
Take no pictures.

This is today's line.

JOURNALING AT THE CAFÉ

I wander a museum of language
while your brown hand rests
in the moment on a cup in
The Ivy on West Street and Litchfield.
You write a postcard
to our daughter.
I take a selfie.

This fog never seems to change
its sublimation
of water-coloured ghosts
beseeching other forms
not to speak
something more
nothing less.

IN BACK OF THE WOOD SHED

When I was a boy
golden and new
I wanted to write blood
poetry so angry I could drag it
out behind the wood shed
so we could kick
the shit out of each other
big yellow moon
laughs
her own precise
verses crunching
under foot

CARLOS

Small crack
of morning
dogs quieted
fattening black bear
lumbers along the treeline
where the blueberries we picked
for breakfast
used to be

TO SLEEP

Simple grey moon over
the yard of January
late winter evenings bundled
in the sleigh to take you
    nowhere
drifting off
anywhere

we wandered the school yard
dark still
greying Patches in tow
eyes golden and guarding
you, the other lullabies
another small ritual
carved in snow
    melted
by a spring you don't
remember

LINE

Out of chilled rivermuck
mergansers pull reeds
roots nourish
flight-weaving wings
the fall winds
another home

On the deck, I remain
single malt loosens a skein
releases a child shadow
beside the shaggy stray
we've kept for years

The river swells
her edges unravel
small drops in my hands

Mergansers launch
a tear
under the
surface

The sky grows another shade

SHELVED

Between a *Red Rose* tea box
of lead net weights
and an *E.D. Smith* jam jar
with four worn sewing awls,
    a china blue teacup -
four black bear teeth
yellowing in the bottom

your fish shack
a library
I cannot read

LIGHT HOUSE SHADOWS
(for Moosum)

Eight-mile channel carved
to feed the hydro dam
water beats forward a stilled rhythm

fur-trade trippers long-passed
awakened souls,
a fisherman on shore

between ribs of an upturned yawl
you mended nets on the rock
long past their time

wind-shivered yellow grass sweeps
white caps sway
water blending colours

killdeer's *ki-ree ki-ree ki-ree*
broken wing protector dance
cast your grand-daughter's shine

tired spring your daughter sips
old afternoon wood smoke tea
canned milk memory dips into surface
returns this fisher to the soil
in their small hands safe
the knots you tied by water

STALLED

May chills your feet
tripping the path

to some version of heaven
you wore through

the dust of winter darkness
in still light settles

instruments of grass
shake off ice
morning empties
its shining glaze

spring, a promissory note
shimmering its silver surface

a cormorant black
on brown stone
stretches in grey wind

OCTOBER EDGES

Jack pine torn below
ragged October squalls
scatters needles
sharps flats
points severed

the trunk broken
bridge finger tips glazed
catch notes
in hungry ice,
clatter through dry channels
what can't be heard
sings still

BENSON PARK

Black elm across yellow moon
       divides that simple night in two
       your side
           and mine.

Restless leaves argue along the gutter
       under smoky neon
       seep from that warm Italian cafe
          off old Stafford.

Timbres in water-coloured streets
       whisper drops
       of the thinnest dreams
          settled in the cracks.

Tourists in our own memory
       we severed ways
       left better selves under the transom
          of that patient wood.

Carved with silent tomorrows
       we promised to write
       (but not to each other)
          pasts peeled like scabbed skin.

You write librettos for the homeless
          on the second sleeve
          of your tired heart
                    studied the sound of variable numbers.

I write grocery lists of ransom needs
          grow thin a wake
          smoke too much –
                    an autobiography by another author.

Seasons faded unkindly
          on the same streets
          of different cities
                    red river gumbo still stuck to my boots.

Your name a blurred smudge
          grows a slow membrane
          over declining Novembers
                    nothing remembered perfectly.

Behind my painted window, still
          you danced in golden rooms
                    my silences behind glass.

Stalled, I stumble, conjuring Leonard and Marianne
          in a stranger café, see that autumn
          from a distance in a frame
                    a box of dried words.

Today, I release old hostages
          the solstice shudders slightly
          every ghost works overtime
                    in the last lines of a poem.

Does that elm forgive us its carved scar?

BIRTHDAY LETTER

Today grief stills,
a spring rain come too late.

Between feeding birds and dusting snow
off the tricycle on the stone walk,
in a smaller now,
I read about your hanging, second-hand,
in an online newspaper.
Suddenly, it is winter, 1985,
and we are smoked out,
fuck-drunk in a bachelor suite
on Hargrave Street.

You are bruised knees, coal eyeliner,
Hank and Purdy looming over a desk:
my refuge from Woodbury's Romantics
class on stormy Menno-nights.
Shedding obedience for submission.

I was my grandmother's K-car, a Legion bursary,
green corduroy jacket, four chords on my brother's Yamaha.
Your head in my lap, speaking through grey air,
drawing you naked,
I followed your voice, licked clean
a thin skeleton of frost
clinging to the window. Witness.

You hated Christmas Day more than any other family holy day:

Birthdays are owned only by those close enough to forget.
Everyone marks the appearance of the Christ,
even shifted to the solstice, to save the pagans.

Mother drunk by three, Uncle a twisting of tongues
carving his prints into your memory,
Aunt – skittish, childless, jealous and cutting
Rumour truths, lies in shadow:
>   *That little missy has been handled more than a Queen's*
>   *Bench bible and by about the same quality people.*

She never knew what she knew.

Tearing off familiar borders,
you became the first to go to university
the first to drop out.
You kept fish on the night stand over the radiator
because they need you but they could not touch you.
Through the steam, walls wept
water too thin to sustain.
Smoked out, we woke late,
another verse hanging on our breaths.
We became opportunity lost,
a paradise of Annettes folded over.

I heard you married and then,
for good measure,
married again.
You needed to change names.
I still searched the book stores for you,
and then,

for lesser measure,
art galleries, record stores, cemeteries.
I moved north. You became mail, occasionally
– a card after the birth of my daughter,
another from Bourbon Street,
your long silence dreamed
I wrote.
We painted new the long art of waiting,
grief like secrets you overhear.
Singled out, you took back your name,
peri-mortem.
Only your uncle attended your funeral.

Today grief stills
after the feeding of birds,
a note perched on the tongue of a grosbeak –
a shiver of red in a misted morning,
your 50th -birthday card
waiting in my desk.

Spring grief tomorrows
crack old husks.

MEMORY NOTES

Open window
lazy accordion plays late
afternoon breath sticky
brown skin warms to nude sky
the air melts tones,
exhales a thick breeze,
a wordless song rising
fingers my neck
dissolves
in you

MISS FERN HILL

The shiniest maybe off a stage of don'ts
the way you stood, cap cocked crooked
before you took
my hand to dance

All through sixth grade
I drew you in tiny red
knotted in the bottom corner
of every green page in my cours de français
Hilroy notebook

Acquainting myself
with little origins of devotion,
truth dropped its penny
between us
            you knew young
            you would never grow old
the shimmering weight of your head
soft imprint in my young shoulder
your voice a small ornate wound in me

Weeks trading night spit
between match lights we picked
our remains out of the spaces
between garden stones
played hide and seek long
into the dark. So small

I would never find you
in the garden over the fence
above me in the tree
the sky in your fingers
between shadows of breath
I envied you until October

red and shining
fading green
you hid outside
your bone cage echoed
laughter without tears

following you out of grace
I have made a tedious adult
I tire of not finding you
untying red knots
into a song of innocence
in the bottom corner
of an empty page

LEARNING TO PRAY

So, I may die properly,
I must learn to empty all worry
retrieve clattering words
from the night

pulled from our shadows
I will not undo
my unravelling
breaths searching
under those same stars

passing light
if you unlock this door
you may discover a poet
(what do you expect?)
but the words are full
the grief is pure.

181 STATION STREET

Seven decades three generations, The Valley Bakery
marriages, graduations, births, two divorces,
the last funeral
a year of plywood windows,
next bakery closed seven months in
two years municipal storage
then for the youth and the old
a pizza joint & dry cleaners
together two winters, a summer between them
then quiet two more years
Grace's Tea Shop & crafts,
(handknit, functional, decorative)
gone by autumn, the sign hung still
four years, eight months littered by
cans, feral cats, an old *Tribune*,
until a high school down
the road rented space Adult Ed
a year's promise then

two but not three
so, Grace's daughter rented videos,
sold crafts again
mostly handknit mainly functional:
the videos did okay
almost four years
but no DVDs then Netflix
another funeral
three years empty
a community development
plan and the last nine months
an Ethiopian teashop
flat bread
Eshe's handwoven crafts
language classes
Tues/Thurs eves
no cost, no credit

WINDOWED

She meant no harm
sitting at my window
while I charted changing hues
falling moonlight on gathered skin.
It never really mattered
if I was there
or not.

If so,
she made love to me.
If not, she made tea,
sat at the window.
I like it better there
most days.

I asked her once what she saw.
Clear glass, she sighed.

One evening
alone she threw a cup
pierced the window.

Now, I wonder if all she saw
then was a piece
of the cedar
outside

before she
outgrew this poem

VOICE

The thin wire of my father's voice
stretches the morning
out like a local paper.
He catalogues the recently dead
gives the crop report
relates the freedom
of a new hip
new corridors, old neighbours
even as this virus keeps him
contained.
Memoried thens,
each morning the same
comfortable new place.

We drink coffee
in different rooms
trading names, old neighbours
catalogue the newly born.
It is the small hours to which
we return best.
Your mother loved
the smell of autumn burning.
Do you remember the name
of that old spaniel?
I listen to the same stories
differently, an old voice
at the other end
of his life.

FORGETTING

Faithless
cold night hangs
alone over
the deck asks me,
Poet, what is your name
for the weight of rain
falling on stars
swimming in a river
below?

SHELTER PRAYER

(for Cory Blood)

Between homes, Gerard Street, September, 1987 –
through weathered loneliness
we walked indigo shadows, night's tongue
traced along the base of my neck
a thin damp film, summoning spirit.

Under the lazy city cement folds
Conklin Shows carny IDs
in our back pockets,
Players Light, eighteen dollars and change
Zanzibar matches

We prayed, as some do
in fits, when the song falls
or the moon slips
past the city's orange hand.

Study the night's light, you said, she holds life
not the web of stars that guided a history
people who came with the land

This night is warmed stairwells
where after hours
security lets you sleep
or
warmed stairwells
where before hours
security doesn't let you sleep
this city a hole your territory fell into.

That hour of sky we cannot name
trembles these empty lots
no starved gods to save
the faithless
wind, crying – dream again
stretch the night
to let a little of the dark out.

And then, you vanished –
NO, no

after, following behind
safe but not saved, I believed
you lived among dark saints
but only your glitter
discarded on badly drawn borders
remains, the smell of smoke in your hair
your voice, your story
a strand of beads broken
spilling under every
things pause

I go back
I go back
and just outside the street light glow,
another thin child
shadows her own
name

a stillness yet to speak
the moon slips
silence I unlock
in prayer to night

ISOLATION

Community shut down
April snow falls again
and we bicker with the distant online
and most fragile scrounge $200
to curl up in a bottle
in rooms we do not see
in rooms we hide

Community shut down
we bake again, make stews
roast hams, moose, fry pickerel cheeks
gather laughter in board games
and old movies, kitchen songs
in rooms we do not see
in rooms we feel

Community shut down
and mail collects
tax seasons, dues, promises
the laid-off search balances,
something to believe in
in rooms we do not see
in rooms we miss

Community shut down
news on a screen, visits on a screen
midnight goes underground
two faces two paces apart
May snows again
in rooms we do not see
in rooms we collect

HOUSE PRAYER

The night after the broken nose
mama sat Ivy down
told her they should pray
for guidance.

Ivy took in a stray
like taking in seams of Kookum's old parka
for comfort, a better fit
a layer against the outside.

One, she named it Help.
It wanted to come when she called
mostly it shook
cried, wet the carpet
avoided Him
licked away her tears
while still Ivy prayed.

After it messed in His shoe
Help disappeared
as she knew it might.
So at night, across the river,
she opened a window
a small glowing moon
a hole in the dark
for us all to see

MAPPING

Cartography a bad joke,
topography below lines,
River and Lake
are not distinct bodies
There is light and dark,
water, sky and land,
pastures and wood,
presence and void

History, a chorus of tales
visits who we have been
under so many coats, skies, words
taking up spaces
printing
in the earth
we planted

LEAVING

House empty
we leave nothing,
next to nothing, take roads
long, straight, narrow,
marked with purpose
void of distraction save
the ridge of forest against
expansive blues ancient greys
striking greens, playful purple
peals of a raven
pressing against
a wind that sounds
as though nothing left

HOMEBOUND

Like a last line of Cohen
Pavlov writes from English Bay
What are you going to do
with what's left
of yourself?

In more restless times
we were actors rehearsing
growing old in elegance,
second-hand fedoras —
before a child, mortgages, *Talisker*
Prufrock's bruised peaches, coy smiles
coy smiles lining shelves we no longer read

Meet me by the pier
this false creek
in your Tom Waits blazer
we will have black coffee, and the sky
will see us both through
again

No line to catch me today
I do like this brightly coloured place
the checkered cloths, the carved chess board
the girl there with cinnamon hair
but no, the woods, a river deep call me now,
the city just a smaller thief

My bones dance their way back
tomorrow, an ash of breath
whispers home
and I will
I will

WORD SHADOWS

Behind the wood shed
where the sun's fingers miss
ermine slips through a gap in the snow
Weasel, you say, pulling the old brush
Stoat, I clarify, leaning on my rake

We've gone on like this for years
bickering behind the wood shed
weightless shadows of words
the snow melts slow
the brush piles

KINDLING

Born in the summer
of a summer's small town,
the sturdiness of trees
their same story of change sustains
seasons darken
and light
       drifts
pulp dries in hollow veins

Aging leaves and needles
collect around cracks
hardened edges softer
evening remains
in a cold house
me burning pieces
of trees
I've come to know

IN THE PORTAGE

Sun dogs over
abandoned wooden skiff
crumbling under lazy
wet snow, her broken keel
cracking March ice
collected
in her grain

Skandics, a tundra
that old *Bearcat 340* rumbled
in heavy frost, cigarette smoke
ski doo exhaust the blood iron taste
back sled hitch pin between
my teeth

Wrapped
in a *Leafs'* jersey
your ashes rest
against an axe handle
the kettle
and the curve
of that damn dog

THE LESSON

i. Spring

after class, supper sun
skims ice-edged water
no plane again today
radiator hums

Marie hums
in squeaky pink rubber boots
red plaid hunting cap

electric baseboard cracks
library radio calls community bingo
chewed *Styrofoam* tea cup edges
pile –

angle vectors learned by *Crokinole*
scraped knuckles
line up

eyes through rough black bangs
        you are my third teacher
        this grade

off the bumper
centre hole ringer
crooked smile kettle whistles
waiting for sister to come
to take her home

ii. Fall

half a moon behind
church steeple shivers
brown eyes brown eyes brown
eyes blue
hall radio moans soft gospel
red ribbon between fingers
30-year-old Marie
places a stone in my hand
closes her teeth
around only the wounds
she can say

> *this is the second cousin*
> *we've buried this year*

in the grave yard I take
my turn carry the shovel
through un-surrendered earth
a silenced language drifts
waiting for sister to come
to take her home

BOUNDARIES

Section 6, Persons Entitled to be Registered
identifies two classes of Indians:
    6(1) - those who can pass Indian status to their children
    6(2) - those who have Indian status but cannot pass their status
          to their children

A good settler, I
review the Indian Act
because a government
still
calls my daughter
an Indian

This Act is not the only mechanism
to determine who may pass
status to their children
Mary's sister will not pass status to hers
we will have to make up the rest
of Jerome
a story unfinished

Harvested trees burned off
    roots remain
soil turning over basalt
muskeg holding on to
a stream under ground

The falling sky
its own city of souls
songs and not songs

I hear

TIRED HOURS

Little spent months slide into timeless passing mist thickens
almost snow drops onto Fischer Ave electric lit evening half
moon slung over train tracks near the beer store sign growing
small she walks same tired block each hour cold wet from
my motel I watch her walk the hours

I know her knew her first left home at 15 second attempt at
high school the clearest edge dimmed by bits of broken past
rumours a family death third time came went edges worn taunted
not from here aged out of care in June can't stay no more
eighteen with grade eight maybe

High black truck slows headlights flash drives the same dark
block cold wet minutes pass my room I step out to the motel
walkway light a cigarette stare down the truck passing time
stares back I am nobody she only a thing an hour is all
that matters to high black truck tonight

I should call her name but I don't call her name tonight
I have nothing she wants no escape no offer I am part of
the broken past I don't want to be passing her time her
passing time she pauses pulls her hoodie up looks my way
high black truck slows lights narrow gaze through me

Small prints in new snow eyes down both of us look no where
for reasons no one knows she asks for a smoke I can smell
the confessions of others on sherry breath prints of tired
hours walked she is smaller now more child than adult less
drop out than student you okay I ask quietly

She takes my smoke looks around unzips her hoodie before me
small bare brown skin asks if I'm okay I look at the ground
between us no I'm fine that's okay she nods zips up
the hoodie shrugs glances past me I say stay safe I say
listen I say her name stay safe okay I say nothing else

She looks up frowns can't tell if she remembers I'm not
just a guy in a parking lot in a tired hour someone
with nothing to teach her she doesn't ask for change high
black truck is gone another block she says thanks for
the smoke you stay safe too we touch hands she walks away

Text my daughter text her auntie text my wife the moon
slung over the train tracks text her auntie hear
footsteps in the snow the dark the silence no prints
are left this tired hour I check again check again text
her auntie no nothing rounds the block this hour text
my daughter

FALLEN VERSES

i. August

After school I found you prone
below the picture window
broken purple finch
in your hands
two hearts shudder apart
silent sobs
swallow divided air

Later, you leave him
for the trees

ii. September

After dusk
I joined Jerome's uncle,
held his sturdy lean shoulders
sharp edge, frayed, unravelling small cords
he cut the boy down from the tree
sudden give, hard embrace
to mute the fall
bodies fold to
gather

iii. October

After 2am, the city phone dies
You are on Ellice Avenue
nothing in your hands but
inherited darkness,
my name, my silence
wandering the night layers

Cut the fruit,
remove the seed,
old story stalls
unstitched ends dissolve
I can do nothing now
but remember
your might

RECOVERY

Last piece in a sequence
our braided kin remains
so many stolen seasons spilled
street scenes, spent rails,
so much empty wilderness,
too many funerals
not enough prayers, restless spirits
burning in brass bowls
We decide time is not just

A container to be filled –
Here we are. You are here. I am
now. Founders slip through holes in
the glass. History shedding its skin again
almost fall more than spring
summer loosens its grip.
We believe time is not

Running to remain still –
Here we pray our braided kin stay
forgivens within nations lost ground
souls distillations purifications past
all those tiny storms collected
and then suddenly finally
it is Step 1.
We discover time is

all we have –

where is the place
just another turn up the road
and if not there?
then, the next turn –

SONGS FOR DAUGHTER

i. *Nitayhi aski*
(the heart of the earth)

mid-summer rain tapped
slow a half sung
ballad, the heart of the earth

grass dancers swept the ground
circles dawning in the drumming,
threaded the smoky August air

you snuggled between us
(your mother and me)
slipped into a dream
as the sun began its yawn across the sky
I carried your kindled bones to the truck
wondering if you were still woven
in the grass, the drums
dreaming circles in the heart of the earth
in your Moosum's sky

ii. *Oski kiskikow*
 (new day)

fading waves of goldenrods turning for us,
in the afternoon sun.
I collected the wonder
that travelled across your face
settled into those brown eyes
as you passed a lady bug
from leaf to leaf to leaf,
summer straying to autumn off the path
green waters and fading blue sky
carry a September
growing wise to us.
I wanted to paint your smile –
your sudden song of 'oh'
as she took flight from your perch –
to hold forever you letting go,
your watching her journey, budding
while I began to write yours.

REMAINS

If you read this
it will always be 3:30 am
the last line waiting
by a box of collected stones –

you are away
I am here

we wait to hear
from each other
we wait

and the words
endure

THROUGH DISASSEMBLED HOUSES
OF PERFECT STONES

Remain one place long enough
the past may leave for another
more suited to memoir
        a song to follow
drawn from earth surrendered
old mornings creep up trunks of ashes
shiver young hours out the veins of leaves – settle
waiting to fasten to new stories

It was harvest when you first left home
seasons collect, telling nothing

Faded ghost, follow that old settler road
off the Yellowhead to an almost-town
where once a quilted history lived
behind shattered windows
        a tourist in its family album
toothless, grandfather's house
cries for her scatterlings
a season out of step
years eat the memory out of history
        shifting seeds drift
scrub trees take back ground lost
land which now forgets how to yield
seasons collect, telling nothing

Wildflowers thinly dusted
fallow under hushed breezes
quilted years
strips of lives straying through ribbons of indigo
mingled in old letter words shared
          each voice holding place
making there here
the weight of history lies
on the spine of memory

… all history is translated